GW00703453

First published in Great Britain in 2002 by
ANCHOR BOOKS
Remus House,
Coltsfoot Drive,
Peterborough, PE2 9JX
Telephone (01733) 898102

Copyright Contributors 2002

HB ISBN 1 84418 030 1
SB ISBN 1 84418 031 X

ANCHOR BOOKS

NATURE'S BEAUTY

Edited by

Sarah Andrew

FOREWORD

Anchor Books is a small press, established in 1992, with the aim of promoting readable poetry to as wide an audience as possible.

We hope to establish an outlet for writers of poetry who may have struggled to see their work in print.

The poems presented here have been selected from many entries. Editing proved to be a difficult task and as the Editor, the final selection was mine.

I trust this selection will delight and please the authors and all those who enjoy reading poetry.

Sarah Andrew
Editor

CONTENTS

THIS GARDEN OF EDEN

These immortal births the sun conceived
    The firmament wonders in boundless skies,
    The moon, the stars, like golden eyes,
Above the clouds a cleft the moonlight made,
    I watched with a joyous heart her lofty ways -
    As crowds of stars around her plays,
Immortal and indomitable around heaven she strews,
    Gracefully rotating in celestial space
    In solemnities of morn, with pleasing grace,

The high church portal opened wide,
    I heard the organ loud and clear
    Whose tones reached out to my eager ear,
Mingled with fragrance in the tranquil air
    Drooping its beauty in the blue of the night,
    Earth's boundless grandeur waiting the light,
The horn'd moon, its splendour receding,
    Cluster'd around - her kin the stars
    Like pendulous lamps in silver jars,

This garden of Eden, this rich content,
    Tender as the deeps under the roseate sky
    In the morn, in the noon, and the eventide,
Clothed in summer vesture in the evening air,
    The clouds were pure and white, the stars came through
    Like trembling diamonds on glistening dew,
Lulled by the coy moon this fair world - adieu,
    When I in such a place, I sure should pray
    That nought less sweet might call my thoughts away.

John Leighton

MOTHER NATURE'S PERFECT DAY

Awakened by a brilliant glow, filtering through my window blind,
To thank the Lord for another day, instantly comes into my mind.
Just a short prayer in the morning, my next move is to get from my bed,
to photograph this magnificent sunrise, of brilliant gold, orange and red.

Enthralled by this panoramic view, only nature can produce such
a sight,
a February morn has broken, yet from Chatteris town not a glimmer
of light.
The sky is looking like a chart, from vapour trails illuminated by
the sun,
when rising from below the horizon, it lights up each and every one.

Such magic moments are short lived; daylight diminishes that
raging glow,
But not to be disheartened, nature has already prepared another
great show.
Just pause for a moment and listen, the dawn chorus has got under way,
The birds of the air sing loud and clear, denoting the start of
another day.

Many birds leave these shores in winter, flying miles with hearts
a-throbbing,
but not the Blackbird, Thrush and Dunnock; and of course our friend,
the Robin.
These are but a few of God's creatures, which remain with us
throughout the year,
find time to feed them every day, you'll be telling them they have
nothing to fear.

This clear blue sky of the afternoon, is a stark warning of an
impending frost?
Nature's way of letting us know, many delicate plants could so
easily be lost.

In the west the sun sinks slowly, the remaining daylight won't
last long,
but high overhead the unmistakable sound, yes, it's the Skylark
in full song.
The sun disappears over the horizon; the sky is a blaze of colour
once more,
As day is transformed into night, nature puts a bite in the air that's
quite raw.
Reflecting on the wonderful things we've seen, before going to bed
we pray,
To thank the Lord for what we have had, during Mother Nature's
perfect day.

Wenn-The-Penn

SNOWDONIA

Along through lush green countryside,
With gently rising distant ground;
Down quiet and bending country lanes,
The air so full of rural sound.

Cloudless skies of the palest blue
Silhouetting far horizons;
Scattered farms and distant churches,
Give to the eye new dimensions.

Approaching now Betws-y-Coed,
Nestling there amid the trees;
Astounding falls of Capel Cerrig
That seemed to put the mind at ease.

Tinge of autumn on turning leaves,
Prelude of rainbow colours bold;
Though distant yet, Mount Snowdon climbs,
Still rising 'mongst the rocks it holds.

Slopes all round with rocky outcrops;
Distorted shadows 'midst the green;
Wandering sheep, gorse and heather,
Make everywhere an artist's dream.

Higher now, the encroaching slopes
Of looming Snowdon's distant height;
Such beauty in its ruggedness,
An overall fantastic sight.

Silver streams with rushing water
And tumbling white laced waterfalls;
Tree covered slopes reaching upward
That lift the sky beyond recall.

H Val Horsfall

THE SEA

Over they spill, those sprayful waves,
As endless as infinity.
Who else could have planned it so,
But a being of Divinity.

In summer they are calm and clear;
Sunshine warms the spray.
Winter's waves are huge and fierce,
With colour, cold and grey.

Above it all, the seabirds live;
Struggling to survive, as ever.
Watching for their daily meal;
With cleverness and endeavour.

Year in, year out, the sea continues,
With its endless moving.
Pounding shore and rocks alike,
As if its might it was proving.

For thousands of years it has shackled mankind.
Each race to his own private land.
Created by a loving God;
By the power of His mighty hand.

Denis A Walsh

SMALL GARDENS

Small gardens are such fun
Takes little time to get things done
Make use of space, do not crowd
Then when finished you'll be proud

Fill the borders with many flowers
To enjoy for hours and hours
Find a corner for those vegetables
The taste you'll find incredible

Don't forget the compost heap
Makes gardening very cheap
Rich in nutrients the garden needs
But never forget those ghastly weeds.

Now it's done take a long look
It was worth the time it took
To get this garden into shape
Enjoy to the full, then shut the gate

Penny Money

OH HILLS

Oh hills, I remember you, stretching out for many a mile,
you have suffered in your life, and still have worn a triumphant smile.
Were you once a scene of battle, was your green drenched with red,
were you there to guard the living and did you also cradle the dead?
Have many hooves pounded over you and guns and cannons boomed,
and were you once adorned in colour when many poppies bloomed?
Have lovers taken their lives on you, or merely ran away, to hide
from a world that won't understand, nor listen to what they have to say?
Have children rolled and played on you, running happy and free,
now that the world is at peace, when man fought for liberty?
How many Spitfires spiralled from the sky,
brave pilots destined, alas to die?
Oh hills, I remember you, stretching proud, across the land,
Standing brave for your call of duty, remaining green,
keeping everlasting beauty.
A thousand years, and even more, you have seen it all,
and remaining on your dignity, you keep on standing tall.

Wendy Diann Steward

DAISY GOES TO CHELSEA

The American next to me at the Garden Centre
Asked for some daisy seed,
It got me thinking about that bright little flower
Many English think is a weed.
Of the times I've carefully put nail through stem
Linking them into a chain,
The expressions on bedecked children's faces
As they want it 'made again'.
It reminded me of picnics on grassy hills,
Daisies nudging the blanket's edge.
Homemade lemonade, sharp and refreshing
And fruit cake - a lovely wedge.

A favourite dress was patterned with this cheerful bloom,
It felt good when I put it on,
Snow-white petals, gold centres - even in rain
It seemed that the sun truly shone.
While watching exotic blooms on a Flower Show
Admiring the wonderful hues,
A garden appeared quite old fashioned,
Its contents making the news.
'We have here a natural environment,
Unstructured - so loosen up.
Wildlife will really appreciate this
And it stands a good chance of a cup.'
Centre stage was a drift, like confetti,
Daisies were having their day,
'So sit back and let the daisies grow.'
Just as I heard the man say.

Mary Jelbart

ROAD TO CHICHESTER

Take the road to Chichester
through England's greenest green,
smooth hills like breasts upheaving
a sight that must be seen.

This England is my England
so full of glories past,
sailors viewed this landscape
to sail before the mast.

Hot fields of golden stubble
cool trees of deepest green,
black rooks that strut the roadside
to peck for grubs and preen.

Yes, this England is my England
and yours I'm hoping too,
so keep this land as always
the place for me and you.

Michael Rowson

THE MOUNTAIN

You stand so majestic, proud and high
Your summit is reaching into the sky.
The trees on your slopes are not very tall
And higher up, there are none at all.
There is just bare rock covered with snow
Even in summer when it's hot below.
Many a climber has conquered your top
But it's hard work on the way up.
Often we do not see you for low lying cloud
Which wraps itself round you to form a shroud.
Sometimes, though the sun is shining above
The view to the ground is completely cut off.
You can be a danger from time to time
With rock falls and avalanches it's unsafe to climb.
You are a symbol, beloved and revered
Though in the past you were shunned and feared
They thought that evil spirits dwelled there
And witches and werewolves were everywhere.
But now we know better and what we see
Is your free spirit and majesty.

Lisa Wolfe

THE STOW ROAD

Gentle landscape, mist muted hues
Long straight roads and far away views
Tall seeding grasses at the road's edge
Ancient stone walls, no sign of a hedge.

Down over Wiltshire's huge grain filled fields
That farmers are hoping will give good yields
Red poppies are scattered between the oats
Rabbits live here, and weasels and stoats.

No need for a map, there's Stow's tall tower
Marking the spot with lasting power
Oft times it's wild on this high Cotswold road
Especially when lightning flashes explode.

Open and free this old Drover's way
With fields of oats, wheat, barley and hay
But on a fine day, spirits rise high
Swallows and swifts and skylarks fly high.

W Dedicott

NATURE'S MEDICINE

If ever life gets you down,
Walk in a wood, and look around,
There's natural medicine to be found,
Follow a river's winding way,
Carpets of bluebell, and field of hay,
Turn blackness into a sunny day,
Leaves and flowers, of assorted hue,
Walk on earth damp with dew,
Aromas of bittersweet fungi-musk,
Blend with acorn and beechnut husk,
Nature's medicine, all of these,
Squirrels run up into trees,
That sway gently in the breeze.

Hear the trill of a songbird,
The sweetest sound ever heard,
This prescription, a walk in the wood,
Guaranteed to make you feel good,
Not tried it yet? Well you should!
If you try it you will see,
Better medicine could not be,
A prescription that works, natural and free,
It's the one that works for me.

Sheila Walters

IRONBRIDGE

Plucked from medieval poverty and rural charm,
Where once was song of bird and scent of flower,
This countryside, uncharted and unknown,
Revealed within its hidden depths - a nation's power!

With man's discovery, here, industry was born.
In one decade the valley's face was scarred
By furnace fires that dimmed the sunset's glow;
And silence rent with din from foundry yard.

One thing remained the same, unchanged -
The river Severn with its floods and shallows,
Beyond control, though spanned by bridge of iron,
Could still, at tempest's whim, the laden trows.

Finally, this untamed source of nature's might
Had proved too strong for man's achievements gained;
And so it was that in the final hour
The gorge was once more silent and unchained.

So now, when many years have come to pass,
And nature's canopy has softened rock and ridge,
Again the peaceful dale attracts the crowd
To learn the history that once was Ironbridge.

Alex Polaine

WOODS AND MEADOWS

God gives pleasure by the hour,
With the glory of his flower power.
God's love echoes in the meadows and woods
and my heart with peace and contentment floods.

In the countryside let me be your guide,
For many of the flowers in the tall grasses hide.
Like the violet, the harebell and the greater stitchwort,
In their own little world a battle of survival is being fought.
Their daintiness is a charming almost fairy-like picture to behold,
And their delicate shades tint the grasses when their flowers unfold.
Such a contrast to the strong Spear Thistle and the bold
yellow dandelion,
I watch the butterflies hover and settle on the much loved red Campion,
Which mingle with the bluebells making a wonderful combination
of colour,
The meadows breathe life into so many popular flowers of which
I never tire.
In the woods and meadows higher and higher the honeysuckle
and wild rose climb,
Decking trees with delightful perfumed garlands displaying
a cascading vine.
Their fragrance wafts on a gentle breeze and I don't know anyone
it doesn't please.
Plants and flowers live in their own little world with their own
sweet vibrations,
Attracting insects from far and wide, knowing there will be
an open invitation.
Hanging bells of the foxglove provide nectar and shelter
from a summer shower,
I find it delightful to watch a big bumblebee take advantage
of this generous and welcome gesture.
Always I am charmed by the magical melodies and the musical artistry
of the birds,
Man copies their serenades for no sweeter music can ever possibly
be heard.

When my time is free the woods and meadows beckon me,
A little bit of heaven in the making, which I find fascinating.
Nature in all its glory inspires me to look and listen, and I am filled
with joy, peace, contentment and love for all God's creation.
No place would I rather be than the woods and meadows
that surround me.
I feel God's presence in the air of that I am forever aware.

Elizabeth Myra Crellin

TREES

Trees! Oh how they comfort me, they are full of grace and mystery.
They speak to me of times gone by; they sway and dance as I pass by.
I listen to their song and chatter and earthly things don't seem to matter.
Their roots lie deep in solid ground, as my thoughts go swirling round
and round.
Oh that I might compare myself to thee, to be a part of your mystery.
Oh how my spirit would rise and be: forever dancing, forever free.

Elizabeth Tanner

AUTUMN BROWN

Translucent wings glide underneath terracotta coloured leaves –
They dip and dive - in and out of falling autumn
While searching for rich nectar
Before the winter snow falls.

Opulent colours - borne on the wing
Blend nicely against the dull browns and greys of moths
That hide behind lavender and late flowering shrubs.

Pot pourri smells; lurk in the shadows of the late afternoon sun
And mingle with my herb garden.

While

Young butterflies - just hours old
Hardly seem to fly - they just float
To wherever the breeze takes them.

J M Stoles

SUMMER SEASIDE

Golden sand
Water looks so calm,
Oh, what a glorious day.
Throwing of a beach ball,
Sandcastles build ever so tall,
Adults soaking up the sun,
Children having lots of fun,
Small boat on its own,
Sailing across the ocean zone,
Lying on the sand,
Trying to get a golden tan,
If it gets warm,
To the water people swarm,
Jump in with a splash
Waves coming around with a flash,
Playing in the sea,
It's everything it seems to be,
Water lovely and cool,
Children acting the fool.

Marie Coyles

NATURE

Spring brings blossom pink and white
Hanging heavy with scented delight
The bulbs are turning to flowers bright
Yellow and pink as they struggle for light

Summer sees the floral displays
Heavy with perfume that lasts all day
Pots of colour in splendid array
Sunbathing in glory not hidden away

Autumn drifts by with trees getting bare
Leaves float down turning in the air
Crisp with golden colours they wear
Skipping on the breeze without a care

Winter is harsh cold and bleak
Animals and birds for food they seek
Iced over waters for many a week
Snow when it falls so soft and sleek

Nature in all its glory abounds
Beautiful landscapes all year round
Seasons for all with sight and sound
Nature with its beauty astounds

Linda Corbin

WONDROUS LOVE

God is within me,
And all living things.
He's the silver on the Birch,
The bird on the wing.

Made he, the butterflies,
The flowers and the trees,
The dew of the morn,
The fish of the seas.

There is nothing on Earth
Or in Heaven above,
That God has not touched,
With his wondrous love.

Marian Lacy

THE SPIDER

I saw a black spider
on the wall.
It was very big and fat
but it wasn't tall.
I looked closer
and it didn't enthral,
however, it had great
capacity to appal
so I put it in the bath
where it performed the crawl.
Then I put it in a box
and showed it to my friend Saul.
Saul was sitting on a chair
in the hall.
He was very thin and tall
and he spoke with a drawl.
He agreed it had great capacity
to appal.
So we took it to his granny
who was drinking tea
and wearing a shawl.
She wasn't pleased at all.
Take that thing out of here
immediately, she said,
or Rentokil I will call . . .
So we went to the pub
and played table football.
Saul got into a brawl.
The landlord began to bawl
and the spider escaped
through a hole in the
skirting board.

John Short

CULTIVATING NATURE

Tamarisks bow to daisies below,
Their feathery pink foliage always on show,
While nearby Laburnum display golden chains,
Against fir trees of pine wood fame.

Camelia and Rhododendron reach up high,
They also 'catch' many a roving eye,
Cultivated in gardens, not merely a weed,
They are there to be cared for,
Whatever their need.

The Oak and the Ash trees,
The Willow and Lime,
Are there to remind us of the essence of Time,
Time as now, or Time past,
Time is forever
And Time will last.

Hazel Sheppard

THE EARTH, THE SKY AND THE SEA

When the combine harvester drives round the fields,
What do the field mice say?
They squeak to their friends,
You must run for your life while you may.
There's a monster running around near our homes,
It must be an unknown species,
If we don't get away right now if we can,
It will just chew us all up to pieces.

When a Concorde speeds across the air,
What do the birds all cry?
Down into the trees friends, down into the trees,
Yes into those trees we must fly,
There's a giant eagle above us, racing
Right through the cloud.
I just do not think it will care about us.
The noise that it makes is so loud.

When those oil holes are dug way under the sea,
What do those poor fish think?
Swim far away friends, swim far away,
Our food here will all die then sink.
Something's polluting our water,
We'll find it so hard to survive,
We must all swim away,
Just as far as we can,
If we all wish to stay alive.

Nita Garlinge

DANDELION'S LAMENT

Down country lanes and in the fields,
In gardens and on lawns
With brilliant lemon petals
And spiky leaves adorned
We stand erect and proudly -
So unwanted, even scorned.
They call us weeds and if we die
We never shall be mourned.
We're never picked like flowers
Or admired like daffodils
But when transformed to parachutes
Float freely o'er the hills.

Enid Hewitt

WE WENT DOWN TO THE WOODS TODAY

We went down to the woods today,
To feed the squirrels and ducks.
We thought they might be hungry,
So we took some bread and a bag of nuts.

The ducks were busy swimming
And eating other people's bread;
So we hunted down the squirrels
To offer them our nuts instead.

We sat and waited quietly,
For a squirrel to appear.
And sure enough - when he smelt the nuts,
A grey one came up near.

We offered him a nut or two,
Which we threw upon the floor.
We hoped he'd see we were his friends,
And come back again for more.

He scurried back, his tail up high,
His whiskers twitching sweetly.
He picked up more nuts with his paws,
And buried them quite neatly!

He then came back a little closer,
His confidence we'd gained.
He took the nuts out of my hand,
Quite a stock he'd now maintained.

The time had come for us to go,
We parted best of mates.
I hope to see him soon again,
I admit, I cannot wait!

Tina Reeks

TWILIGHT CHARMS OF A HEATWAVE

To see and feel my dear England in her finest cloak
Beyond the garden by the pond I sit on the old wooden seat
With my loyal stout friends the tall Lime, proud Beech, strong Oak
To enjoy the cool stillness of twilight after the day of heat.

The balmy silence is broken by the lapping of my dogs as they drink
I cast my eyes heavenwards to the mellow oranges, yellows and greys
Tracing the sky after the roaring red sunset as Phoebe sinks
Taking with her yet another of our precious God given days

As the dusk hovers the water before me yields many clues
Of its residents, the feeding fish safe from the heron's sight
The pond skaters scurry the surface in their tiniest of shoes
And the drinking bats enchant me with their spectacular flight

I love these rare moments of true mid summer upon me
To count my blessings and be awash with such calm
Glancing at the silhouette of the huge leafy tree
All the hustle and noise pleasantly gone from the farm

Who is roaming beside me? It's mamma hedgehog
Scavenging the grass leaving her footprints in the dew
She may roll to prickle my inquisitive dog
In the stack yard she'll sleep when tomorrow is new

Curfew for the tired birds I've heard announced by the owl
The podgy badgers will check soon on the wasps' nest nearby
Sly trigging foxes abound but roosting safe are my fowl
And the darker it filters pure twinkling stars jewel the sky

Time fore me to rest, I feel contented with nature's late charms
I rise, the sweeping garden looks beautiful even in the gloom
The open-windowed farmhouse welcomes me with familiar safe arms
I will sleep soundly tonight under one sheet in my warm room

Jean Williams

Sugarmill Woods, Florida

Great wood you are ageless and timeless
Your shadows steal over the earth
Creating fantasies, shapes and pictures
With your passion for living and rebirth

Tall pine trees shelter ferns and palm grasses
Woodpeckers, red cardinals delight in your stare
Your magical bird songs thrill as we ponder
Blackberries, small insects, butterflies galore

Sunrise creeps silently through twisted branches
Spanish moss drapes eerily over the trees
Making great sights of perfect beauty
Pine cones sit proudly challenging the breeze

Such magical moments that nature shows us
The breathtaking beauty fills us with awe
Special thoughts that live on in our memory
We can dance in the ageless wood ever more

Elizabeth Hunter

THE BLIZZARD

The blizzard raged relentlessly across the huddled barren plain
And tore at the bulky clothing worn by the man who struggled in vain
To keep his legs moving though buried in snow right up to the knee
He knew that he could not go on fighting this storm, and what his end
                                                                would be

He stopped for a moment to adjust his big pack
Looking from side to side, but never looking back
By now he was suffering the full extent of exhaustion
And was aware that he had no choice but to improve his position
He forced himself to get moving again, into that wind and
                                        blinding snow
And found himself wondering why he had decided to go
On this perilous mission with conditions so bad - and worse still
                                                        to come
Was he going mad with such indiscretion to take on this journey - ?
                                                he must be dumb!
He uttered a curse, and shook the snow from his coat
And looked around for some shelter but saw nothing of note
So with a prayer on his lips he strode out again
In the hope that things might improve - and then came the rain!

Len Corner

THE BEST THINGS IN LIFE

A meadow full of buttercups,
On a lovely summer's day.
A gentle breeze,
To soothe life's cares away.
Butterflies of many shades,
To enchant, to please the eye,
Bird songs all around,
To lift the spirits high.
A babbling brook,
As it goes on its way,
Scarlet sunsets,
At the end of the day.
The fragrance of a rose that lingers,
On a warm summer's night,
Twinkling stars and a silvery moon
To bathe or world in light.
Just some of nature's gifts,
For you and me,
No labels, no bottles
And absolutely free.

Veronica Taylor

TREES

Oh, what beautiful trees,
Blowing in the breeze.
Oak, pine and palm,
They all look so calm.

Oh, the wonderful trees,
Blowing in the breeze.
Orange, red and green,
Are the colours of the leaves.

Oh, the magnificent trees,
Blowing in the breeze.
Standing so tall,
And looking so fine.

Oh, what beautiful trees,
Blowing in the breeze.
Apples, coconuts and pine cones,
Falling swiftly to the ground.

Oh, what wonderful trees,
Blowing in the breeze.
Everyone being different,
But still looking so great.

Oh, what beautiful trees,
Blowing in the breeze.
Oh, what I would give to be a tree,
Looking so glamorous . . . and free!

Stefanie Martin

MOON MOMENTS

Curtains swaying gently
A moonbeam shining through
Quietly to the window
And all I see is you

A smiling face
Nose, mouth, each eye
You're always there
For me so high

Mysterious and handsome
At times so very round
A friend indeed to all the stars
And for me that's on the ground

Clouds beyond the raindrops
Falling just like tears
Suddenly your radiant glow
That takes away the fears

Quarter, half and sometimes full
At times you try to hide
But never are you far away
You are always by my side

Gillian Ward

MORNING DEW

Ah, Niobe, have you walked this way early?
Your tears are everywhere before my eyes
Scattered on hedgerows in profusion pearly
And on the grass that all around me lies.
Upon each little spider's web they glisten,
And every leaf's a-tremble with a tear;
And in deep silence, awed, I stand and listen,
But, though you weep, it is for none to hear.

Pleione Tooley

RAIN SHINE

Week upon week of grey dreary rain,
rain on the windows and rain down the drain.
Dripping and swishing, rushing and roaring,
brown muddy puddles, waterfalls pouring.
Mists across the fields and cobwebs hang low
beaded with rain, while the cold winds blow.
Driving across the sodden brown ground,
trickling and soaking, no relief to be found.

From behind the clouds, the sunshine beams
changing the world with golden streams.
Filtering through trees with autumn hues,
as the leaves flutter down to carpet the view.
Sparkling berries of red, white and gold,
showing life's plenty before days grow old.
Mellow yellows and multicoloured trees
mix with the greens until winter's freeze.

Hilary M Rose

NATURE IN HER BEAUTY

Oh what a wonder to behold
To see the light of dawn unfold
The pale sky that glows into gold
To hear the birds sing soft and sweet
The grass, fresh and springy at our feet
Cobwebs jewel-like, wet with dew
Blossoms opening soft and new.
The distant mountains purple with shades of blue.
Clouds softly surround them with a misty hue
The lake sparkles and shines in the sun
Another new day has just begun
Now red-gold sunset in a rosy glow
Night time comes gently warm and slow
The indigo velvet sky of night
Stars shine and twinkle, so wonderfully bright
The moons silver pathway the glistens on the lake
Gentle lapping sounds, the water makes
Nature in her beauty she gives so free
If we would only take the time to see.

Christine Corby

THE ATLANTIC SALMON

My life starts from an egg where clean shallow rivers flow
Where I live for more than a year to progressively grow
I then make my way to sea waters deep
Where I will live on the crustaceans I reap
Now I have a breeders' girth
My instinct is strong to return to my place of birth
Many waterfalls I will leap to reach my destination
Where I hope to spawn with a little flirtation
After I have spawned my energy is at a low
I must try to make it back to the sea to continue to grow
Now fully mature my big silver body earns much admiration
I will again return to my place of birth to repeat my propagation
The Atlantic salmon's life cycle is on-going
As long as fresh clean rivers keep flowing.

Brian Bates

BLACKBIRD SONG

Drowsy at dawn on linen pillows,
  Snuggling down in peace and calm,
Never did whisp'ring ocean billows
  Breathe such balm,

As that which melts a May day morn,
  Enthrals the gentle mavis throng,
And opes the organ stops of dawn
  With miles and miles of song.

Their voices brawl the joys of summer,
  Of roses drowned in fragrant dews,
And how one idle summer lover
Laughs to hear the news.

Their poem too at parting day
  Immortalizes lazy light,
Laments the disappearing ray
  And serenades the night.

But do but hark that whistle travelling
  Wildly round some city square,
Just one solitary song unravelling
  Sweetness everywhere.

Terence Belford

THE GREETING OF THE GREEN

When the leaves return
When bare twigs take on the sheen
When sticky buds unsheath green pearls,
When will these wonders be seen?

When the leaves return,
When spring bursts forth with joy,
How can man redeem
The green his greed destroys?

When the leaves return,
When all has a tropical glow,
Those who rejoice at the greeting of the green
In heaven ever green shall know.

Graham K A Walker

NIGHT

As I stand and watch the stars at night
I think of rainbows, and of light,
Of planets many years away
Where dawn begins another day,
Or life exists along a rim,
Between the furnace and the dim,
Worlds of red, blue, brown, grey, green;
Earth, wind, water, grass and treen.
Dragonflies that ride the air.
Mushrooms growing here and there.
Flowers never seen before,
Deserts, mountains, seas, and shores.
Great clouds of gas that fill the sky,
Where every colour meets the eye.

Athol Cowen

MORNING THOUGHTS

As I look around in morning light
my heart sings.
I see boundary trees of varying height
grandest of all things.
Delicately slim or lofty and towering
Trees are my delight.

The dew-damp grass beneath my feet
feels to me so good -
Softer to walk on than any street -
Grown for cattle food.
The early sun creeps up the sky
Birds sing so sweet.

Oh beauty pure where're I look
I praise my Lord
for giving me this morning bright
and memories to hoard.
So, late in life, with failing sight,
they're in my 'inner book'

Jean Dorrington

TRAVELLERS' REST

Rhododendrons bloom, in splendid array,
Golden Laburnum, colouring the day,
Beautiful flowers, in neat little urns,
Freshly cut grass, wherever one turns.

The sun shining down, from a clear blue sky,
Oh! How I miss you, I will till I die.
But here in this place, a peace now descends,
It is somewhere special for family and friends.

The weeping is done, and I smile once more,
You are there by my side, in my thoughts evermore.
All the happiness we shared through the years,
Now drowns the sorrow and banishes the tears.

From the small chapel, singing fills the air,
Voices raised in praise by those who care.
The pain leaves my heart, in this tranquil place,
And I have found peace, with God's tender grace.

Doreen Bowers

THE TASTE OF SALT

The smell of salt upon the air,
waves crash on the shore without a care.
The wind blows cold,
and ruffles my hair.

The feel of sand between my toes,
damp in the breeze tickles my nose.
The seagulls call,
day begins to close.

I love the beach in the evening light,
that special time between day and night.
The time when you
walk into my sight.

The taste of salt upon your skin,
waves crash around us, kisses begin.
You touch my hair
and give me that grin.

The feel of sand underneath me,
your warm touch, a love that's meant to be.
A heart that soars
then crashes with the sea.

Deanna L Dixon

THE BUSY SPIDER

Dew drops glisten on the silky web
Stretched across the leaves
Lacy patterns of the finest threads
The busy spider weaves
Watching with her tiny eyes
Waiting for unwary flies
Tangled in this sticky trap
Beating wings, making gaps
Alas there is no escape
Even if the strands may break
Darting quickly for her meal
The struggling insects soon will feel
The stinging pain of that fatal bite
As she swiftly takes them out of sight
Eagerly she starts to savour
The tasty fruits of her labour.

Doris Lilian Critchley

Rain

Dry, parched earth opens hungry jaws
To swallow welcome rain, that pours
Along the gutters, into drains
Sweeping the roads and washing lanes,
Causing fast temporary floods
On land unable to absorb.
It swells lakes, rivers, ponds, small streams,
And to each dried-up bed it seems
As though there'll never be enough
To satiate their appetite.
Rain hangs in dew drops from the line
It drips in rhythm, beating time
Till windy gusts disturb the flow,
Cascading waterfalls below
And languid plants revive again
Their thirst quenched by life-giving rain.

Rosemary Webb

NATURAL OBSERVATION

I walked the cliff top path, on a mild, pleasant summers day,
Looked down on the rocks, gliding gulls, fingers of spray.
Switched off from issues that tax, conditions of pay,
Wrapped in silence, the caress of the breeze transported my cares away.

Above the dwellings, far from the drone of vehicles on the busy road,
Expanse of country, solitude, privacy, greenery, animals abode.
No lingering steps, noisy distraction or effort to think
Never allowing one's good mood, cordial spirit to sink.

Along the disused railway line, old quarry workings,
                               now pasture for cattle,
Remains of the past, derelict gun emplacement, ruined fort,
                               scene of a battle?
Flowering plants, fertile fields, shelter of hedges, majestic trees,
Thank God for beauty, delight of senses to savour moments like these.

Rich blue sky, fishing boat, a tiny mark on the vast volume of sea,
Quote from the hymn 'Hath stabilised it fast by a changeless decree'
While a busy farmer on his tractor works hard on the land,
The incoming tide, controlled by the moon, reclaims, covers the sand.

For many miles I hiked, enjoying the freedom, inhaling fresh air,
No noisy printers, impatient phones, artificial light to circulate its glare.
Absence of material progress, schedule, deadline or dull care,
No buildings to obstruct, chimneys pollute or splendour impair.

I stood for a moment, contemplated, gathered the impressions I felt,
Digested and froze them inside so they would not melt.
Returned to my starting point, left 'nature's realm' far behind,
One I can only recapture, replay, in the depths of my mind.

Stability.

Dennis Overton

I DREAM

I dream you take my by the hand
Far, far away to an unknown land;
Where green fields and mellow hills
Are fringed with jewels of daffodils.
Where blushing borders of roses anew
Flaunt velvet petals of vibrant hue.

I dream we tread the woodland ways
When autumn leaves are all ablaze
And burnished sunsets long dusk rays;
Into my eyes with love you gaze.

We walk until the sunset glows;
Where the wild wind-flower blows,
The air is chilled and no bird sings,
Only silence the woodland brings.

When twilight beckons, then homeward bound,
We tread the silver-frosted ground;
Just you and I under star-filled skies;
I dream of you and Paradise.

Annette Barker

Morfa Bychan

Our children enjoyed this seaside,
Where ribbed sandbars trapped the ebbing tide,
Leaving salty warm pools ankle deep
And exposed seashells as tokens to keep.
The scattered sun danced on aquamarine,
To the rhythmic lapping of waves serene.
Giant castles rise fleeting to the sky
Where wheeling seagulls with effortless lift fly,
Which have escaped the clinging limpet rock
And tangled brown seaweed to join the flock.
A gentle sea breeze of fresh mingled airs,
Soothes away a few of life's wrinkled cares,
As all who have smelt this briny bouquet,
Will be refreshed and remember their stay.

Andy Joiner

ODE TO BROADWATER

The rising sun salutes the day,
As night shadows quietly flee away.
The awakening birds in mist surround,
O'er tranquil water, bear their sound.
Oh beautiful valley, a treasure you hide,
As the waters open, Mother Nature has cried.

I sit in awe as the midday heat,
Brings heron and dragonfly, out to meet.
A flash of silver, out o'er the water,
The ripples spread and one to the slaughter.
I turn around and see bulrushes dancing,
Or is it just otters in wild romancing.

A reflection of wonder in water so still,
Slieve Croob masked, o'er McKinstry's hill.
The rippling sky, as they meet together,
To split the spire, before clouds gather.
Owen sleeps peacefully, beneath the scene,
Oblivious to beauty of everything.

Alas, the westerly willows stretch their wings,
And darken the water as nightingale sings.
A black and white stranger, from Friar's glen,
Shuns cunning neighbour from out the den.
The sightless night birds and wise old friend,
They all appear at the long day's end.

Memories of barges and horses she holds,
And echoing voices of long gone souls.
Old Geordie Weir, I can hear him call,
His night boat drifts slowly, up the moonlit hall.
I think the Lord for a beauty to hide,
The Broadwater now sleeping, by my side.

Stephen James Bann

KING OF ACORN, KING OF OAK

Old oak tree standing tall,
What wisdom of the forest walls.
Oh such stories might you tell,
Ancient yet strong and weathered well.
You feel the rain and the bright shining sun,
Jack Frost as he bites after autumn's done.

Your roots that push into the depths of Mother Earth's womb,
The lovers by night whom shelter under your branches,
The whispers of passion by the light of the moon.
Your leaves bright, green, golden brown by fall,
Fertile acorn bursts, becoming drinking cups for the fairy ball.

You are a safe resting place,
There you stand for furry friends and feathered flights,
And the little magical folk of the night.
King of Acorn, King of Oak,
You nurture the needs of all who come.
Dear Oak tree, all nature's assets you have in one.

Natasha Faiers

TERESA GREEN

Sitting in my garden, the sun shining down on me
I wonder what it must be like, to be a tree.
My feet in the earth, my face to the sky
My arms being perched on by birds passing by.

As autumn approaches, there's a chill in the air
When I should be dressed, I find I am bare.
But as the warm weather comes heralding the spring
A bright green overcoat is what I'm wearing.

I'd see such a lot standing twenty feet or more
Instead of just being a lowly five feet four.
Being stuck in one place might become mundane
To move I'd have to uproot time and time again.

I'd no loner need creams, my youth to retain
You never see a tree trying to smooth out its grain.
No more fears of the therapist armed with her wax
Only the worry of a gardener wielding an axe.

No more trips to the hairdresser, to be perfectly groomed
All I'd need once a year is to be gently pruned.
I'd wear blossom, have leaves, and even bear fruit
But in winter I'd shiver just wearing my birthday suit.

There are obvious advantages in being a tree
But I think I'll remain just being me.
So my daydream of being a tree has now ended
Just happy that all is as nature intended.

Teresa A Tickler

FROST

Shimmering, glimmering in the morning sun,
Bright sparkling colours like a butterfly's wings,
Silently changing the bare brown twigs,
Into beautiful patterns.

Touched so softly, left undisturbed,
Except for the fluttering jewels moved by the breeze,
Soon gone as the warmth from the sun descends,
There but for a fleeting time.

Barbara Martin

SCARLET DANCERS

Summer foliage green and lush
Olive, emerald, copper blush
Majestic pines and aspen trees
Faded gorse on sandy screed.

Silver birch and sycamore
Later, seeds will clothe the floor
Hazelnuts are disappearing
Squirrels' ritual summer clearing.

Intermingled in-between
Elderberries' bright lace cream.
Shining Laurel strikes a pose
Next to Alexandra Rose.

Poppies drift between the corn
Scarlet Dancers start at dawn.
Buttercups splash yellow paint
In amongst the Queen Anne's lace.

Pendulums of weeping willow
Fields of rape in golden yellow.
Paint box colours, brightest hues
Mixing cornflower's purple blue.

Firs of glorious evergreen
Pointing fingers in-between
Fans of rowan, larch and oak
An abundant heritage of hope.

Elizabeth Cleveland

THE HUNT

Horses hooves thunder down upon the ground
The dogs bark loud and gather round
Bright little eyes peer out from the bush
Birds fly up to the sky with a rush.

The countryside is all of a quiver,
While tall trees sway down by the river
The little fox looks out and hears a loud shout
Down to the earth he goes.

The hounds linger round and smell the ground
Following the huntsmen with horn blasting loud
Into the wood they go
They look back and are gone with the pack.

Wendy Sims

THE DRAGONS OF SUNSET

My eyes were filled with golden fascination,
as I gazed upon the splendour of the sky.
I saw the gleaming sunset's fiery dragons,
upon their evening journey passing by.

As I walked, between the pine trees they darted.
Their radiance glowed as fire on stream and hill.
They glimmered, till they faded on the waters' ripples,
The wonder passed; the eventide was chill.

Dorothy Mary Allchin

FLOWERS

Daisies grow in the garden
They sprinkle the lawn with white
In rain or lovely sunshine
They are a wonderful sight.

We have a little Daisy
She grows each day in our heart.
She's going to be very precious
With her we'll never part.

We'll have to water and feed her
Just as a garden bloom
But 'twill be a glorious pleasure
She'll chase away our gloom.

Whether she's sleeping or waking
Shedding a tear - perhaps or two.
We'll always love little Daisy
In grey skies or in blue.

D Adams

NATURE IS A WONDERFUL THING

Nature is a wonderful thing.
As trees burst forth new green leaves
It's then we know that it is spring.
The birds fly with twigs to built their nests.
Sparrows, blackbirds and thrushes sing.
Flowers start to peak through the earth
With their pretty blooms in the breeze swing.
The sun which, for so long, seemed to sleep
Shines for hours in a sky of deepest blue
Whilst the rain no longer makes us weep.
Little lambs frolic in the new green fields
And farmers sow seeds in furrows deep.
Rose, daisy, the sunflower yellow
Camellias, lilies from new buds peep.
Summer passes in a pleasant hue
With holidays spent by a warm sea,
But soon autumn appears on cue
Offering its colours of gold and red
And harvest time gives a lot to do.
The reaping of crops ready to store,
Now daylight hours will seem too few.
The trees all too soon their leaves shed
And wintertime's around the corner;
The animals know it's time for bed.
Among fallen leaves upon the ground,
Snow falls cover what seems to be dead
But it is only time for sleeping
And soon all will rise again their heads.
Isn't nature a wonderful thing?

Joan Earle Broad

LITTLE BIRD

Oh little bird a-watching me
From the safety of your tree.
Ever searching for some food
To feed your hungry nestling brood.

Are you a spirit from a far off plain
Come to dwell on earth again?
Were your feathers angels' wings?
Your song the tune that heaven sings.

How proud your speckled little breast
That singles you from all the rest.
Are you a messenger from God above,
To tell the world about His love?

Where do you go when night's curtain falls?
Do you sing when Jesus calls?
Were you there at Calvary's tree,
When He died for you and me?

Did your voice lift Mary's heart,
When from her child she had to part?
God gave you flight so you could guide
His saviour son back to His side.

Oh little bird a fluttering there,
Fixing me with beady stare,
Thank you for alighting here,
Bringing our creator ever near.

Sue Ireland

COUNTRY LIFE

I love my cottage in the countryside
The landscape rolling far and wide.
To sit in the garden in my favourite chair,
The smell of the flowers filling the air.
A skylark flies off from the meadow nearby,
Singing so sweetly as it soars in the sky.
The sheep in the pasture all sheared and clean,
It really is a lovely scene.
Watch the cows all munching the lush green grass,
Give a casual glance, when people pass.
See the sun set behind the hill
The evening is clear and quiet and still
Hear the hoot of the owl as it calls to its mate,
Heard by the mouse, alas too late.
Bats flying round at an alarming pace,
As if they are in a relay race.
Catching food for their young in the cave,
To save them from an early grave.
Dawn breaks in a misty light,
After another long and lonely night.
Once more I sit in my comfy chair,
The day looks set to be sunny and fair.
I look to the sky and gratefully say,
Thank you Lord for another day.

Les Whittle

A Long Lost Dream

I walk in silent solitude, along the country lane
The hedgerows look so fresh and green cos' spring is here again
The ripple of the water from a tiny brook near by
Did someone whisper to me? I must be dreaming! Why?
Because I've gone back to childhood with an old familiar scene
Though many years have passed since then, this perfect place to dream
I hear the voices of the children, while they play happily and gay
With their laughter and their shouting, no cares to mar their day
I sit upon the style a while to recall my long lost dream
It was so long ago, though only yesterday it would seem
Across the meadow yonder, grazing cattle and some sheep
In the distance I can view a forest with tall firs and pines
Do they really reach the heavens or is this my child-like mind
Then I realised that nature had not changed at all, though I was beguiled
God still created all this scenes for young and old to see
Just the same as when we were children, yes! And absolutely free
The happiness of a childhood dream, was a treasured interlude
Recaptured in the country lane, on this walk of solitude.

Williamina Gibb

SEASONS AT THE RED MILL

Winter's mantle, and icy streams,
Water wheel still, cold moonlight gleams.
The robin's eagle eye, and ruddy breast,
Tells all, that nature is at rest.

Spring at the Red mill, and all is waking,
The water wheel, starts shuddering and shaking.
Sending its froth and bubbles into the moving stream,
And the watery sun now sheds its beam.

Summer's here, with a sky of azure blue,
Yellow throated daisies, and butterflies new.
Magnolias and rhododendrons bloom,
All set to chase away winter's gloom.

Autumn creeps in, with mists and dew,
The trees lose their leaves of red and gold,
Rose hips and berries, show their colours bold,
The mill is peaceful now, as summer bids adieu.

Red mill by the stream, water wheel in flow,
A boat floating near, and the river banks, put on their show,
The trees are dressed in splendour, regal and serene,
The seasons fly past here, an ever-changing scene.

Anne Roberts

IN DEFAULT

To please you, I'm to set the wind to verse!
Have you at all considered what you ask?
Of subjects, there could scarcely be a worse,
Of writers, none less suited to the task.

To start with, there are few good rhymes for wind,
At least, not many I can bring to mind -
The time is past when one could have began
Without affectedness to call it wind.

And really, d'you expect me to find new
Extollings for its virtues now, you dunce!
Don't you remember an Odd Oder who
Said all there is to say of Westers once?

I wrote you several verses in the past,
To demand more of me is more than rude.
This balmy day fosters an icy blast -
You know what's said of man's ingratitude!

I'd soon, were it embarked on, be at loss,
Becalmed in seas of silence without shore,
Almost as if *I'd* shot an albatross -
No poems scattered, Frosty, on the floor.

So better note this down, now and for aye,
That I decline to write upon the wind.
I'm sorry, but that's all I have to say,
And if it's in breach of friendship, well, I've sinned!

Patricia Morgan

NORTH SEA PRAYER

A light stands, lonely on the Suffolk coast.
Where, now Friday's catch is off the boats,
With sea-salt tears and bitter brew,
They raise a toast to a missing crew.
'To the great dark sea,' passes quiet from lips,
That have drunk too often to local ships.

'May nets run deep, and holds be brimming,
And silver fish come our way swimming.
Oh God protect this ship of mine,
And let my sons see out their time.
And dear Lord if I should drown,
Take me quickly, when you take me down.'

Robert Paul Cathmoir

I See

I see the sea through a sunshine weather.
I see a faded line that goes on forever
this is the line that meets the sea
this is the shore where the sea meets me.

I see the sky that's all around me.
I see the clouds I'm feeling free
this is the time when there is no time
this is the rhyme, a moment in time.

I see the shore through a rock window.
I see the shore change with a water flow
this is the beach where the people lay
this is the hotel where the people stay.

I see the boats through a sunshine view.
I see many colours on an oblong of blue
this is the picture I hang in my mind
my mind is a gallery I see what I find.

I see the people through postcard eyes.
I see the shadows through sunset skies
this is the time when sky and sea are one
the colour is black the boats have gone.

James B Woods

THE DAFFODIL

Oh dear, it's dark and cold down here,
The ground's so hard and winter's long.
I wish Jack Frost would disappear,
The trees are bare, the wind is strong.

But joy, the soil is soft at last,
I hear the birds sing in the trees
I'm waking up from my long sleep
To feel the sun and gentle breeze.

My shoots grow stronger day by day
As up and up they gently creep,
Now I have leaves and one small bud
A little flower begins to peep.

I have a pretty yellow gown,
A daffodil for all to see,
I dance about so happily,
Oh thank you God for making me.

V Cox

RESPECT FOR THE EARTH

To catch a glimpse of a dream, to make a new start
That vast environmental issue which engulfs us, must take its part
About 150 years ago Chief Seattle spoke inspired words of truth
That every creature and part of earth was sacred, nothing uncouth.
To destroy nature and its wonder, was to destroy life itself
Are we beginning to realise as we hear of the world's health.

We discuss the environment close to home and town
Animals have nowhere to go, because of the trees being cut down.
Foxes living near homes to scavenge from dustbins for scraps of food
As wastelands are being built on, as suits the council's mood
Mountains in Wales are being destroyed for road foundations
Disfiguring the countryside that has been there for generations.

Where do we fit in and who are we as consumers
For we take everything we require, as vulnerable customers.
In Peru and Boliva, people live simple lives like explorers
Discovering how to use the river for their daily adventures.
To fish for food, to keep clothes clean and for bathing
Using trees and herbs for medicine and not destroying.

God made man and all that grows and lives on earth
He gave us the privilege of naming all creatures that give birth.
Our stewardship in caring for His creation is paramount
For future generations our conservation will account.
We benefit from all the discoveries in the past,
And we must ensure our generation is not the last.

Inner feelings say that to go back to a simple life is not the way
For man needs to progress by discovery in work every day.
To learn more about the world and its part in the universe,
Inventing new techniques for saving life and limb, we must not reverse.
Our dream is for a shared responsibility to preserve the earth
For the greatest gift that God gave us was our birth.

Ralph Andrews

I'D LIKE TO BE

I'd like to be a little frog
Ex tadpole - sitting on a log
Beside a cool and shady pond
Until some princess waved a wand
And turned me into someone grand
A prince, the finest in the land.
I'd leave my ugly froggy wife
And live a truly handsome life.

Daniel Jack

THE CALL OF THE SEA

I can hear the call of the sea
The wavelets say come dance with me
As they lap gently to and fro
It's in my heart this I know
That I was meant to sail afar
And have my own guiding star
At dawn the clouds then unfold
And the sun makes me a path of gold
The sea breeze comes with fragrant air
And I gaze at the blue without a care
The seagulls glide up on high
On gentle wings in the cloudless sky
The ship is gently sailing on
Now the seagulls are all gone
From the stern of the ship I look to the wake
And wonder how long the journey will take
Then I can hear the roar of the sea
I wonder what she is saying to me
As I listen quietly there
Where the billows cause a gentle stir
Now they whisper unto me
Can you hear the call of the sea?

Margaret Bate

BEAUTIFUL ROCK

I'm standing at the water's edge looking out to sea
My head is slightly heavy I know what it can be
I hesitate as I stand there wondering what to do
But I decide to go for it the sky is very blue
I'm swimming out the sea feels good against my heavy head
I swim for the rock that's sitting on her water bed
I climb up and lie in her glove like hand
Breezes touch my body as I look out to land
The sun shines its heat as it streams down on me
I feel so relaxed as the sea caresses me
Rushing up and down then gentle as can be
Healing my burnt ankles with the ripples and the flow
I feel we are one together and this she does know
What beautiful feelings sweep over me
As I am one together with the breezes sun and sea.

Janet Skinner

DEW ON AN EARLY ROSE

I walked along the garden.
The air was quiet and still.
My eyes went off to a distant scene
Of sheep upon a hill.

The birds were not yet risen.
The foxes were at home.
Looking at my garden,
I felt no need to roam.

Dawn shone on the roses
With their dewy stems,
While violets and lobelia
Adorned the borders' hems.

Cob spiders' webs were shining
In the rising sun.
I stood and watched as it rose,
And saw the day begun.

Roger Tremethick

NIGHT

Darkness, greyness, murky phantoms in the shadows creep
Blessed indeed are those who sleep.
Not for them the wearied sighing of unyielding twisted sheet,
Nor cramping cry of knotted feet.
Horrors, fears and nightmares craze the enfolding walls,
Bizarre cacophony of calls;
Tears and sweat scatter lonely myrrh across the dappled way;
Impossible to pray.
The ticking clock sends time backwards, or so it seems,
Hallucinating dreams.
Muffled sobs escape from pillows now cling bunched up on the floor,
Tingling every nerve wracked sore.

Why is it that dark can be such a haunted demon thing?
(Yet the nightingale will sing).
Is it that Circadian trapped we're anchored in the muddied tide,
And nowhere can we hide;
So here we have to face what light can sometimes push away,
And starkly in array
The nooks and crannies of our inmost being stand revealed:
But here we can be healed.
As dawn tiptoes brushing forward breathing after night,
The oh so welcome light -
Our naked pain is shrouded in His all pervading glow,
And He has come to show
That He created night for quietness and peace, not fears,
And here with us He bears
Every burden of our guilt. He plucks us from the darkest deep
So breathe in Him and go to sleep.

Priscilla Noble-Mathews

NATURE'S ORCHESTRA

We are all motivated by music
Be it folk, reggae or soul
Some like the classical pieces
While others like rock and roll.

I love to hear all of these sounds
But the music that motivates me
Is the beautiful music of nature
Rich in its simplicity.

Take the dawn chorus of the birds
There's no conductor needed there
Every note is perfect and sweet
As it fills the morning air.

Listen to the grasshopper's rasp
Or the gentle buzzing of the bee
These are chords that need no prompting
They can use them instantly.

The crescendo of an angry sea
The ripple of a gentle brook
All of these are musical notes
Not to be found in any book.

The sound of thunder and lightning
The beating of rain on the ground
The elements' contribution
To nature's orchestral sound.

Christine Spall

THE SWAN

Take me with you as you glide
Where rippling waters sing,
Dressed in down of feathers white
With grey marks upon your wing.

Pass waltzing dreamy daffodils
And where weeping willows spread,
Their tendrils like thin fingers
Along the water's edge.

Take me with you when you fly
Across summer skies of blue,
Graceful as a lone white cloud
Full of the morning dew.

Take me with you as you leave
When the season disappears,
Do you go to a nicer place
Where no man interferes.

Where wildlife is precious
Where no cruel humans dwell,
Then take me with you my dear friend
For no one shall I tell.

Ada Ferguson

CLOUD GALLEONS

Like galleons' sails the clouds sweep by,
Their ocean is a bright blue sky
Beneath their shapes the seagulls fly
   On wide-spread wing.
Snow white or washed with springtime gold
With underneath in contrast cold
Black and grey hulls the wind will mould
   From clouds of spring.

Were those who sailed the western seas
Called from their homes by scenes like these,
No longer thrilled by gentle breeze
   And shores well-known?
And did our island race set forth
From east to west, from south to north,
On reckless quests of priceless worth,
   The seas to own?

You March-born ships, above, below,
Come, let our hearts adventure know,
Again on us the gifts bestow
   Our forbears won.
Let youth and age in friendship strive:
While galleons' sails before us drive
And English daring leaps alive,
   Our tale's not done.

Kathleen M Hatton

A WINTER'S TALE

A whitened world awaits me, as I look from my window
Jack Frost has been busy, there's ice and frost and snow,
The wires are like tinsel garlands, hanging from the poles,
The garden flat and level, as the snow has filled the holes.
Icicles like candles are dripping from the spouts
And winter has arrived of that there is now doubt.

You may think this would make me snuggle down in bed,
And pull the blankets further up around my head
But there is something special, about a crisp snowy morn,
Still, silent and mysterious, just a little after dawn,
You get the feeling, that all is fresh and new,
As if the scene can only be seen and watched by you.

You can see your footprints, across the freshly driven snow,
As you leave your mark behind you, wherever you go
There are signs of life, little trails and tracks.
Left by hungry birds, or quiet cunning cats.

The sun comes up all glowing, like a fireball in the sky,
The snow clouds come over, and blot it from your eye
The wind starts to freshen, blowing snow flurries in the air,
Whipping up the drifts and forming them with care.
A blizzard soon is raging a whirling, twirling sight,
Floating round like feathers, blotting out the light,
I know it can be dangerous, the slush that follows very dull,
But a blowy, snowy morning can be very beautiful.

Joan Atkin

DRAGONFLY

Flash past me now oh breath of light
you were just there, now out of sight
a pleasure to delight the eye
skimming across a summer sky.

It's made it seeks to find
before the day is left behind
and I must wait until next year
to see again that I hold most dear.

J K Williams

AT RUTLAND WATER

I sit by the banks on a summer's day,
With the world a million miles away,
And I take in every fragrant scent
Before the day is finally spent.

Wisps of cloud in a cobalt sky,
Swifts and swallows circling high
Above the cruising Rutland Belle,
That's just put out from old Whitwell.

True beauty is here, there is no question,
From Hambleton to Edith Weston,
And all about this tranquil place,
To soothe the brow of the human race.

And down along the south east shore,
Normanton's church, with watery floor,
Has charm enough to make me say
I'll stay again, for another day.

The butterfly, the fox, the bird,
The fish who tests the angler's verve,
All thrive in this idyllic spot,
That seems to say, forget me not.

Then in the hush of failing light,
The geese arrive in arrowed flight
Across the pink and ashen sky,
To settle in the reeds nearby.

And soon the veil of evening falls
On Rutland Water's peaceful shores,
The darkness, merely to delay
The beauty of another day.

Colin Hart

FRUIT

They nestle in a bower of leaves so nature's palette can decorate.
With colours all can gaze upon; that artists try to emulate.

The luscious Plum, and Grape so sweet; that shades from
green to purple hue,
a powdered bloom rests lightly on, transforming them to silver blue.

Orange, lemon and Apricot describe themselves so very well.
The vividness of these fine fruits; so easily it is to tell.

Take a Cherry in the hand; a thread of stem to hold it by.
Just like a tiny ball of silk. The colour red delights the eye.

Such beauty has the juicy Peach. Its velvet skin a joy to hold.
The colour of this sumptuous fruit - from palest pink to deepest gold.

A glossy Apple, shiny smooth. The colours of its spectrum; prove,
Autumnal - it can be said, from Russet brown to Worcester red.

Such pleasures from this harvest feast, delicious fruit to gratify.
Yet many more than just these few, will nature grow and beautify.

Molly Phasey

DORSET

Home to me is country lanes
A bank of primroses fresh from a shower of rain.
Wild daffodils dancing in the breeze
Under the beautiful chestnut trees.
The smell of wild violets in the air
Gazing over the green meadows everywhere.
Peacefully the cattle graze in the fields
There were horse and carts with old-fashioned wheels.
The wonder of a robin's red breast
To see all the work in their nest.
Listening to the glory of a wild bird's song
To me the country is where I belong.

The simple sight of a country pond
Watching the moorhens wander along.
The colourful mallard duck swims contentedly by
To me this is peace to the eye.
The site of a tractor ploughing the earth
Watching the seagulls fly behind in their search.
Fields of poppies and daisies
Reminding us of those who fought in the war.
The majestic hills of Bulbarrow
With its wonderful views
The grand old churches with wooden pews.
There are picturesque thatched cottages
Standing in a row,
This to me is unique and home.

Aves Swanson

TREES AND THE ELEMENTS

From nowhere, it seems, a gentle breeze,
Passes through and teases the rippling leaves,
Cavorting and twisting in the capricious wind,
Laughing and leaping by the gusts within.
The huge oak stands still in the silence before a storm,
Nesting birds are quiet in the moments just before the dawn.
The rain comes and cascades from leaf to leaf,
Rivulets run down the trunk to the roots b'neath.
When the softly fallen snow envelopes the land,
The willow and elm shiver in their thin coats, and,
Wait for the sun to come out, which warms,
Their leaves, turning their faces to bask in the cosy rays.
Whatever the elements, the trees always give,
Us, beauty, peace and a sense of wonder in the world which we live.

Paula Loveridge

HARVEST HOME

A random truth once hidden from our eyes, can manifest
                                         itself in hidden things;
Circadian circles of the farming year and rainbow fruits each
                                         passing season brings.
That God is good is seen in bread and wine; kaleidoscope of
                                         fruits on which we dine.
Together now, the harvest meal prepare, a token of the
                                         first-fruits that we share.
The gardener plants and weeds until the day, when berries
                                         sweet and stone-filled fruit so sour,
Are gathered in, preserved and saved in store, for winter days
                                         when cooking fills the hour.
The kitchen garden planted row on row, where sun-drenched
                                         walls with peaches overflow.
The ancient vine with clustered grapes entwined, near
                                         cordoned pear and russet apple grow.
A treasury of riches all around, from fields of corn and
                                         maize with bursting cob,
To beans, potatoes, onions, rich red beet and rows of
                                         peas with fresh green pearly pod.
From marrow, melon, mustard, fragrant mint, to chive
                                         and carrots, Swede and curly cress,
While olive, sunflower, linseed, oil seed rape, yield up their oil
                                         abundant from the press.
For nuts and hops and cider apples now, to give God thanks
                                         we yearly make our vow.
Successive crops at harvest take a bow and early seed-time
                                         beckons with the plough.

N Rudge

A Sting In The Tale

Once on an early morn they came,
Huntsmen cantering down the lane.
Resplendent in their coats of red,
An eager pack of hounds they led.
For stirrup cup they had regard
So rode into the tavern yard.

Refreshed and longing for the chase
They set off at a merry pace.
And to the cry of 'Tally Ho'
Quickly o'er the fields did go.
Over lush green sward they sped
To where the wily fox had fled.

The fox then disappeared from view,
Gone to ground near an avenue.
Searching through those trees, they found
Beneath a tree, hole in the ground.
The dogs had clearly caught its scent.
To dig him out the men's intent.

'Can you tell us if he went in?'
They called to a lad with a cheeky grin,
He nods, and so they toiled with a will.
No fox was found but they dug, - until
The lad remarked with a gleeful shout
'I knowed 'E' went in, cos I see'd im comeout!'

D Brockelbank

NATURE

In spring and summer when leaves abound
And grassy tufts cover the mounds,
Many things are hidden from view
That could surprise and even delight you.

So winter is not all bad news
It all depends upon your views,
When trees and hedges their leaves shed
It does not mean all is dead.

As you wander country roads and paths
Do not scorn the winter's aftermath,
Look beyond what was once a screen
There's interest and beauty in every scene.

A beautiful mansion is suddenly there
Where before we thought the hill was bare,
Horses with their shaggy winter coats
Fondled and fed from the moored boats.

A winding river through a field
That once a golden crop did yield,
The river is home to many creatures
And a very pleasing country feature.

June Funnell

BIRD DAY

The morning songs at crack of dawn
Arouse us from our sleep
To tell us each new day is born -
No time for slumbers deep.
With cheerful chirps they swoop to lawn
Or from the branches peep.
Only ring doves sound forlorn
Whilst solemn vigil keep.

Blue tits leave their nests to feed
At tables well supplied
With nuts and bread and grain and seed
And then away they glide
To feed the fledglings all they need
In beaks that open wide.

A coconut hangs from the perch
Attracting finches, robins, too,
Then long-tailed tits join in the search -
With acrobatic posture seeds pursue.
Below the table pigeons land and lurch
Towards the scattered remnants - all too few.

Throughout the day it's such a sight
As blackbirds, thrushes, magpie, crow
Come swooping in and soon alight
And stay until supplies are low.
As early evening turns to night
Day birds leave and wise owls know
The time for them to hunt is right,
And helpless creatures fear that foe.

Maude Newton

SPRING

The blue tits probe the petals
For the grubs that hide away
In the bursting buds and blossoms
That grace the trees in May.

Insatiable the fledglings
Their orange voids present,
While feathered shuttles fly apace
On satisfaction bent.

Like velvet humming tops the bees
Their contribution make,
To all the living sights and sounds
Of nature now awake.

The fascinating hover flies
Hang motionless in air,
Gone in a flash with lightning speed,
Elsewhere to reappear.

Those spangled mimics borrow notes
From farmyard and from moor,
And with shrill whistles stir the brood
To clamour still for more.

And such is spring when life awakes
To clothe the naked earth,
And all creation demonstrates
The miracle of birth.

Douglas Higgins

NATURE

The sun glistened through the golden leaves,
showing silvery spider's webs which weave
gracefully between a mass of trees
swaying gently in the breeze.

Branches lined with wisps of dew
lay fresh, dazzling, just brand new.
Everything quiet and still -
only the wind whistled through.

An owl swooped over, again no sound,
eyes fixed on prey upon the ground.
As fox cubs frolicked around their den
I held my breath in anticipation again
as the vixen passed close by.

Clouds gradually became shrouded in a darkened grey,
I hope the rain won't spoil the day.
The heavens open and down pours the rain,
animals darting for cover again.

Grouse scuttle into gorse and heather,
keeping dry their rumpled feathers.
I glance and spot a fallow deer,
the inclement weather has started to clear
and the sun begins to reappear.

A shimmering rainbow starts to unfold,
I wonder if there is a pot of gold?
This natural beauty charges no fee
always ceasing to amaze me.

A flock of birds overhead fly
I take a deep breath and heave a big sigh
'This is something money can't buy!'

Alison Jane Lambert

MY PATCHWORK QUILT

I sit on the hill and look around,
I cannot believe what is on the ground,
For as far as the eye can see
A patchwork quilt it must be,
Browns and greens, yellow too,
And those colours are just a few.
A few black and white dots I see
Its cows and sheep amaze me,
Contented they must be
To live a life and free, so free
God made these fields to plan
To work it out, I must if I can,
Keep people at work on the land
Animals happy with their life -
God wanted fields to be like this
And give everyone his idea of bliss,
So much comes from the Earth
To keep us alive, it does so much
And all because of God's gentle touch.

Kathleen Patricia Peebles

YOU ADD FLAVOUR TO MY LIFE!

When I was introduced to you,
You were in pieces, cut up, dried;
Yet life took on a flavour new
When adding you to food I tried.
Of all the herbs I test and use
It's you that I most often choose.

I did not know how you might grow
When I planted a pack of seeds.
As the young shoots began to show,
At first they looked like common weeds;
But, testing leaves by taste and nose,
Your fragrance from these plants arose.

Soon you were grown, and fit to pick
A few leaves for my daily wants;
Leaves soon replenished, growth was quick,
You became vigorous, luscious plants.
When autumn comes, before you die
I'll choose best leaves, to keep and dry.

Then, through the winter, I can store
Some of your fragrance and fine taste.
To me you're precious. I'd abhor
Letting your goodness go to waste!
You add such subtle flavour blend
To many a meal - Basil, my friend.

Nancy Solly

AUTUMN

The wind it will blow
and cause a small breeze
and the leaves will start
to fall from the trees.
They come in all colours
yellow, brown and red
to the ground they will fall
make some animals a bed.
Slowly they fall
like a bubble of air
and all of the trees
begin to look bare.
Animals collect them
and start to make beds,
they are going to hibernate,
get down their sleepy heads.
Children throw sticks
into the horse chestnut tree
they chant a rhyme
'Drop down you conkers to me.'
They fall to the ground
all covered in spikes,
they split them open
to play the game they like.
So all animals asleep
all the leaves have fell
everyone is ready now
for the long winter spell.

Heather Dunn-Fox

THE SEASONS

The autumn leaves that fall and fade
The trees look bare and cold,
Along the paths the leaves are laid
Their colours brown and gold.

Then winter comes the wind and snow
The leaves are swept away,
Leaving the earth with such a glow,
The sky so full and grey.

Spring, it comes, new joy it brings
The earth with joy awakes
The flowers, the trees and birds that sing
A wondrous scene this makes.

The summer sun, so warm and bright
The days are longer now.
Greens, yellows, reds in sight
Erupting with God's power.

John Young

FLOWERS OF THE FIELDS

An English midsummer, with skies so blue,
Fields crowded with clover of red or white hue,
Honeysuckle, dog roses, clambering high,
Sweet little violets, half-hidden, shy.
Primroses, cowslips, thousands of daisies,
A-peeking from grass with tiny white faces . . .
Dandelions too. A glorious glow,
As all their yellow faces show.
Looking skywards to the sun,
To bask before his race is run,
Staring up with faces bold
To make each field a sheet of gold
Earth-grown glory, 'neath Heaven's sun,
Where we could play, Oh, full of fun,
In days when there seemed so few tears,
And as we played, no sense of fear.
To think of growing up? . . . Oh never!
In those days of childhood seemed forever.

John Whittock

LEAVES IN AUTUMN

Waiting for attention
Lining up to die
Fragile in their beauty
Stunning passers-by.

Curling lemon with bright green trim
Orange, red and gold
Lacy coral, deepest plum
Colours growing old.

Waiting for that wilder wind,
Waiting for their fate -
Ending heaped in clusters
By our garden gate.

D Howard

THE WILD ANIMALS OF NATURE

The badger leaves the safety of the set,
Foraging for food that her young will get,
Hopefully going while no one spies,
Then digging them out while she fights and dies.

Mr Fox, the cunning dog,
Leaves his den in the thick of fog,
He runs and hunts for his family meal,
When he returns to the vixen at night,
The young cubs squeal for the food with delight.

The little field mouse going foraging around,
Has to be careful on the ground,
Their little ears finely tuned for a hoot, hoot,
There's an owl about, it's time to scoot.

Olly the barn owl high in a tree,
Looking around for a meal for free,
Is that a field mouse in the corn
Gathering food for its newly born?

Oh look over there,
There's a nice sized hare,
That's more of a meal for me,
Mr Field Mouse you are free!

R Hopkinson

As I Walked Along

As I walked along a country lane
The sun shone through the trees
My hair was blowing around my face
In the gentle breeze.
Far away in the distance
I could hear the cuckoo
As I walked through the grass
Wet with morning dew.
It was a beautiful day
The sun was blazing
And in the green fields
Cows were a-grazing.
I felt like I had walked for hours
So I stopped to pick some wild flowers
I then sat down upon the grass
For a rest but time soon passed.
In the distance I could hear
The church bells ringing
And all around me was
The beautiful sound of birds a-singing.
Now I must be on my way
It really was a lovely day.

Joyce B Campbell

SILVER MOON

Oh joyous moon that shines this night
And smiles down on the child so fair.
Sending spangles glitter bright
Casting silver threads amongst his hair.

Silver is the night
Silver are the trees.
Silver is the boat which
Sails on silver seas.

Oh stars that wink
And shine so bright.
Like silent wishes scattered
Through the ink-black night.

Magic is this night to me
Moon dust on the wind so free.

Moonbeams gaze down
From the clouds
Silver linings glow
Like heavenly shrouds.

As darkness fades, the sky's
Ablaze with burnished gold.
Mystical, magical at an end
As the moon now grows cold.

Linda Jefferies

THE DEEP BLUE SEA

When the light of dawn unveiled creation
the lion's share of Earth fell not to dry land
but to the seafarer's torment - and Poseidon's recreation -
it fell prey to the clutches of the mighty hand
of an ebullient, leonine monster, brusque and tempestuous,
tumultuous, vehement, ferocious, blustering, impetuous.

Yet like a beguiling siren or knavish water sprite
the beast beckons its human prey with beauty untold
as it gently purrs and sways to lure and excite
as it woos and endears before it tightens its hold.
With awesome grace this grimalkin in disguise
flashes its chatoyant aquamarine eyes.

This rippling, heaving, frothing Bounding Main
enchants with an iridescent kaleidoscopic form
of stalking strength and rhythmically bouncing mane,
a polychromatic feline poised to pounce and perform
its cataclysmic betrayal upon unsuspecting braves
bewitched and seized and sunk to their thalassic graves.

O! What can cajole and pacify this beast
with the heart of a sibilant, blue-blooded sphinx
that it should forfeit with compassion its sacrificial feast?
What can quench the thirst of that tsunamic lynx
that it should abandon its displays of tyrannical power
that force its admirers to tremble, despair and cower?

Alas! That undulating, nacreous neritic nymph
will always attract with its teeming life as bait
feigning the innocence of a crystalline lymph
toying with its catch before sealing their fate.
Yet the allure of sapphire, hyacinthine, emerald, kingfisher blue
assures the reverence and wonder this cosmic element is due.

This vast abyss, this rolling, galloping swell
presenting its crescendo as it surfs and stalks and spumes,
of flourishing legends where mermaids and monsters dwell,
this mercurial scalloped sway of moiré silk and peacock's plumes,
this deep blue Sea encircling man, licking and purring as a kitten
blinds logic with its feline charm to ensure man remains smitten.

Efrosyni Hobbs

SUMMER STORM

Distant and deep, the voice of thunder
Scatters the bloated clouds asunder,
Then comes a vivid flash, revealing
Cows in the meadow, seagulls wheeling.

High on the cliff the trees are bending,
Seeking to flee the tempest's rending,
But, like a whip, the wind is lashing,
Sending the tender branches crashing.

Hark to the hail's insistent chatter!
Flowers are flattened, pebbles scatter,
Things that escape the tempest's mauling
Drown in the drenching torrents falling.

Then all is still, the storm has vanished,
Turmoil and strife alike are banished,
While but a zephyr stirs the ocean,
Spent by its recent angry motion.

Washed by the rain, the pavements glisten,
Nature herself would seem to listen:
What does she hear? A lark ascending,
Telling the tale of tempest's ending.

Dorothy Elthorne-Jones

NATURE

Nature bursts into the spring,
As she wears her golden ring.
The mayfly on the water glides,
While kingfishers for fish dive,
All nature at its very best,
Has to pass the final test.
The fields are full of clover,
As the geese fly over,
Honking loudly as they fly,
In formation in a cloudless sky.
They are looking for somewhere
To raise their brood with loving care.
The corncrake with his noisy croak.
Doesn't amuse a lot of folk.
Especially if you live nearby,
Your patience they can sorely try.
The skylark sings so beautifully,
While the cuckoo sits in a nearby tree.
A peregrine falcon way up high
Shows his aerobatics as he goes by.
A stag beetle drops from above
As we hear the cooing of a turtle dove.
All of nature is there to see
And with us for eternity.

Winifred Tutte

THE FOREST IN SPRING - AN IMPRESSION

Tranquillity amidst soft shades in dappled light.
Leaves whispering together whilst out of sight.
Chuckling streams wink at Sol, then trip away,
Elephant skinned boles hold their umbrellas high.

Idle ponies glance quizzically around.
Industrious ants tickle trails on the ground.
Twigs crack, warning vigorous wings above,
Spring buds burst proclaiming the season's love.

But restless mankind ponders and performs
Ruthless evil to this lovely world.
Come Friend, thank God for nature's dignity
Which negates villainous humanity.

Roma Scrivener